JEWEL IN THE CROWN

# Jewel in the Crown

*Bonnie Cone and the
Founding of UNC Charlotte*

William Thomas Jeffers

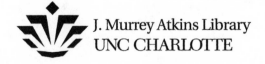

J. Murrey Atkins Library
UNC CHARLOTTE

J. MURREY ATKINS LIBRARY AT UNC CHARLOTTE

Suggested citation: Jeffers, William Thomas. *Jewel in the Crown: Bonnie Cone and the Founding of UNC Charlotte.* DOI: https://doi.org/10.5149/9781469664095_Jeffers

ISBN 978-1-4696-6408-8 (paperback: alk. paper)
ISBN 978-1-4696-6409-5 (open access ebook)

Published by J. Murrey Atkins Library at UNC Charlotte

Distributed by the University of North Carolina Press
www.uncpress.org

# CONTENTS

I first met Bonnie Ethel Cone during my sophomore year, 1988–89, at UNC Charlotte, when she would have been around 81 years old. I was introduced to her by Dr. Loy Witherspoon. "Doc," as he was known to me, had extended an invitation to attend a performance of the Charlotte Symphony along with Professor of Political Science Nish Jamgotch and Ms. Bonnie. That was a night of firsts for me—I had neither attended a performance of a symphony nor ever met the founder of our university. That dinner and concert grew into a friendship that greatly influenced my life.

Later that same year, I would approach Ms. Bonnie and ask her to assist me with a letter of recommendation to transfer to another UNC school, one with a light blue hue just up the road in the Research Triangle. I have told this story several times over the years to the great humor of my friend Phil Dubois, who retired as UNC Charlotte chancellor in 2020. Thankfully for me, there is an element of redemption, growth, and learning from one of the most categorically incompetent things I have done in my life.

Here is my story. I had a good experience in high school, save for the fact that I spent much of my youth as a fan of just one university, albeit not the one that Ms. Bonnie built, and I was convinced that I would receive a full academic scholarship to that other university. However, I learned a very valuable and painful lesson as a high school senior: I thought I was the smartest person in the room, but I was sadly mistaken. I did not obtain a scholarship to that school, and I was very bitter about that. To say that I had a chip on my shoulder would be an understatement; it would be far more accurate to say that I arrived at UNC Charlotte with what looked like a boulder on my shoulder. And then I had an opportunity to meet Bonnie Cone.

Dr. Witherspoon, the former chair of the religious studies department and two-time chair of the faculty senate, was the advisor of my fraternity. I went to see Doc and told him of my plans to put in an application to transfer, which I said I needed to ensure that my application for law school was the strongest that it could be. Then I told him that I would like to ask Bonnie Cone for a letter of recommendation. He just smiled and picked up the phone to call Ms. Bonnie. In doing so, he set me up for a classic and epic fall right on my thick head. Like only a true educator can do, he allowed the child to make his or her own mistake, and the lesson has been set in place for a lifetime.

So Doc and I called Ms. Bonnie, and she agreed to meet with me at the Cone University Center for lunch. So there I was in the Cone Center, where a lovely and large portrait of Ms. Bonnie hangs, having lunch with her (now 81 years old) and asking her for a transfer letter of recommendation. I told her about my plans to attend law school, and she listened quietly, nodding her heading politely, not saying a word. At the end of my presentation there was an awkward silence, a pause. Finally, she said to me, "Mr. Wilson,"—she never called me *Mike* or *Michael*, always *Mr. Wilson*—"is it more important to you to be a part of something that someone built for you, or is it more important to be a part of building something yourself? When you know the answer to that question, come back and see me, and we will finish our discussion about that letter of recommendation."

I had no idea what had just happened. What did she mean? What was the right answer? Would she write the letter for me or not? Then I came to realize that Ms. Bonnie was asking me to consider whether I was a Forty-Niner and would help her advance the university's mission, or whether I was so insecure and shallow that I had to run off to a name-brand institution seeking comfort and protection by obtaining a degree where a number of others had attended before me—almost a cowardly way of trying to find success or validation in a herd of sheep, rather than standing confidently on my own two feet.

I decided to stay at UNC Charlotte, and my friends and I determined that day to work on making our campus—our university—better. In fact, pushing ourselves to be better, I ran for student body president that spring of my sophomore year, and I won in a landslide. I served in that role my junior year, and it was an amazing experience which taught me that an idea, backed up by a sound plan coupled with hard work, can be a positive catalyst for change.

I hope that you will enjoy the glimpse into Ms. Bonnie's life and work compiled and so aptly related by William Thomas Jeffers, as much as I have, and that it will allow the reader in some small measure to know and remember Ms. Bonnie. From those humble beginnings, UNC Charlotte has grown to surpass 30,000 in student enrollment, with more than 100,000 graduates.

Cone rings the Old Bell as she commemorates the 25th Anniversary of the establishment of UNC Charlotte. Looking on is Michael Wilson, president of the student body, who later went on to serve on the university's Board of Trustees.

May this story remind us all to be a catalyst for positive change, to learn, grow, stumble, and fall and begin our journey again. And remember always Ms. Bonnie's vision.

September 21, 2020
Michael L. Wilson
UNC Charlotte Board of Trustees, Chair 2019-2021

# ACKNOWLEDGMENTS

This book is based on the online exhibit, *Bonnie Cone: Educator, Trailblazer, Visionary*, written by graduate assistant Jessica Injejikian in 2013. A project of the Special Collections and University Archives unit of the J. Murrey Atkins Library, the website was created as a celebration of the unique personal qualities that made Cone powerful enough to build a university and better the lives of countless students, faculty, staff, and members of the broader community in Charlotte, North Carolina. The site was created with the support of Madeleine Perez, the university archivist at that time.

A special thanks also goes out to Tina Wright and Edward Perzel, who conducted so many of the fascinating interviews that made it possible to write this book. Sadly, Dr. Perzel, one of the founding faculty members of UNC Charlotte, died in 2020.

This project wouldn't have been possible without the contributions of so many others as well. Christin Lampkowski and Tiffany Davis of Atkins Library's digital publishing services provided their constant support, shepherding the book through the entire process. Stacy Rue, Rita Johnston, Katie Howell, Andrew Pack, and Kate Dickson were indispensable in finding and selecting the photographs. Ryan Miller's design graces the cover. I am grateful also to Somaly Kim Wu, who helped to get the project started, and John McLeod of UNC Press. Financial support was generously provided by Kurt G. Waldthausen.

# INTRODUCTION

## Dawn Schmitz

"She had this dream, she sold it to everybody, and it actually came to fruition." —Loy Witherspoon

THE UNIVERSITY OF NORTH Carolina at Charlotte's origin story is Bonnie Cone's story. Having started her career as a talented educator, teaching the most difficult and in-demand subjects, she went on to steer the development of the institution from a temporary college extension center, to a junior college, and finally to the fourth campus in the University of North Carolina system. Without the benefit of family status, wealth, or even gender privilege, she accomplished all she did through her magnetic personality and by martialing qualities of a great leader: persuasiveness, perseverance, and vision.

It is hard to believe that heading into the postwar era, there was no public university within about ninety miles of North Carolina's largest city, Charlotte. Concerned that many Charlotteans were deprived of access to higher education, Cone made it her life's work to remedy this situation. And she was a force. William Friday, president of the University of North Carolina system from 1956 to 1986, recalled in 2012 how Cone persuaded so many in the Charlotte business community to support the effort: "I think it's one of the most remarkable stories of evolution in American higher education, and I've seen a lot of them across the country."

This evolution began when Cone was recognized as a gifted mathematics teacher and invited to teach at the Charlotte Center, an extension center that was established to offer night classes for returning GIs in 1946. She was the key figure in the transformation of the center into Charlotte College in 1949 and the University of North Carolina at Charlotte in 1965. Through eighteen-hour workdays and seemingly endless trips to Raleigh to meet with legislators, Cone was persistent in moving toward this ultimate goal, continually clearing obstacles and recruiting allies to achieve it. Those closest to Cone, like founding religious studies faculty member Loy Witherspoon, described how she made her vision known to everyone in her presence: "She was consumed with it; she could sell it to the most negative person in the world."

After she had served as president of Charlotte College and played the pivotal role in the university's founding, many in the community thought Cone would be named the first chancellor of UNC Charlotte. However, she was not selected, in part due to the belief that her not having earned a PhD would make it hard to recruit faculty. Despite this, her ability to persuade outstanding faculty to come to Charlotte College and be part of the drive for university status is clearly documented. Jack Claiborne, journalist and former associate vice chancellor of public relations for the university, remarked that upon meeting her, faculty from prestigious universities all over the country "would be bowled over by her, and she would have great success recruiting them." Harvey Murphy, founding kinesiology department chair, observed, "Never before and never since have I been with someone who is as impressive on first meeting as Bonnie Cone." Witherspoon noted simply, "She had an uncanny ability to convince you."

Cone operated on many levels: chief executive, colleague, teacher, and mentor. Even while building a university, she always had time for students. Stories are plentiful of her encouraging or persuading individual students to attend college and finish their degrees despite the financial problems and other hardships they were facing. A story told by Claiborne is representative: "Now, imagine this: Bonnie Cone in her really sort of moderate, mild, and maidenly dresses, going into the *Charlotte News* newsroom—a really tight, smoky, loud, second-floor office on South Church Street—and asking to see the managing editor and then telling him that he needed to hire this young man as a copy boy so that he could earn enough money to go to college." Charlotte College student John Kilgo was hired by the newspaper, completed his degree, and went on to have a distinguished career in journalism.

No university is built by one person. In addition to the many civic leaders, business owners, and politicians influenced by Cone to support the establishment of UNC Charlotte, there are also countless community members, faculty, staff, and students who are part of this story. Most of them have made contributions that are not recorded and thus will never be celebrated, and this story is a testament to all of them. But this year, on the seventy-fifth anniversary of the university's origins as Charlotte Center, we honor and pay special tribute to our founder.

The following pages feature excerpts from many hours of oral history interviews with Cone and her colleagues, conducted between 1973 and 2012 by university faculty and staff, including members of the Special Collections and University Archives unit of the J. Murrey Atkins Library. During these conversations, many of them taking place in the library and in university offices, narrators described in detail the experience of bringing a great public university to Charlotte. These interviews, and most of the photographs, are available online at goldmine.uncc.edu. All of the photographs and other primary sources are available in the UNC Charlotte archives, which are held in the library. Sources used in each chapter are provided at the end of the book.

## CHAPTER 1

# A Gifted Educator

"Dr. Garinger turned to me and said that I had to take over as director. I told him I couldn't, but you see, I did . . . and here we are."
—Bonnie Cone

THE FOURTH CHILD OF Addie Lavina Harter and Charles Jefferson Cone, Bonnie Ethel Cone was born at home in the town of Lodge, South Carolina, in March 1907. Lodge was originally known as Hope until the town's first post office arrived, and the name was changed to avoid confusion with another "Hope" in Lexington County. Since the primary landmark and meeting place for the town was the local Masonic lodge, the new name, "Lodge," stuck. As Cone recounted, her dad had several roles within the town: "My dad had a farm, but he also sold automobiles. . . . In addition to having these businesses, he was the mayor of our little town for years on end."

Cone realized at an early age what she wanted to be when she grew up: "I knew from my very earliest years that I just wanted to be a teacher." A story is often told about a precocious young Bonnie ardently lining up her family's chickens for a lesson, but she dismissed it as poetic license. As she recalled, her journey toward teaching began with a piano. "I remember that I always wanted to play piano," and "I was playing a piano on a windowsill" where "I could just imagine this was the keyboard." When she was five, her father purchased a stand-up piano. All that practice at the windowsill paid off when young Bonnie, who took her first lesson the afternoon it arrived, quickly became proficient.

This eventually led to her first teaching job when the town's only piano teacher married, moved, and, as Cone recalled, "left a lot of disappointed little girls and boys. So the parents of these children came to my mother and said, 'let Bonnie teach our children what she knows.'" This love of music more than likely nurtured a nascent ability in mathematics, because the latter can serve as the foundation for the former, but she did not realize how good she was at math until she was inspired by a geometry teacher after she finished high school.

In those days, formal education ran through grade ten. Although opportunities for college preparatory work were available at the time, they primarily served male students; two examples were Cone's older brothers, who went to the Carlisle Military Academy in nearby Bamberg, South Carolina, to finish their secondary education. While there was never a question that Bonnie would go to college, her father told her, "You know, I think it might be well if you just stay home this extra year." As she remembered, "I went back to the high school, and that really was my best year." She credited the new math teacher, Ed Rentz, with helping her make mathematics come alive. "I saw it as a body of knowledge that I didn't have to memorize, that I could reason, I could use my abilities. . . . I know I owe a great deal to this man because . . . when I got into teaching later, some of the techniques he used were still effective for me on my students."

Cone had her heart set on going to the teacher's college of South Carolina, Winthrop College (now University) in Rock Hill. Her parents, however, were not sanguine with that decision. They thought Winthrop, with a student body almost ten times the total population of Lodge, "too big a place for this timid little girl," she recalled. "Then we considered other places, and they thought then that Coker College, which had in the neighborhood of 300 to 350 people, was a better" fit. Cone received a work scholarship from Coker, grading papers in the mathematics department and occasionally filling in as a substitute teacher. In her senior year, she even found herself teaching the college's own dean of students because the dean "had never gotten a college degree, because she had never had plane geometry."

Cone spent the next eleven years teaching math in the South Carolina public school system. Upon graduating magna cum laude from Coker in 1928, she took her first official teaching position at Lake View High School in Lake View, South Carolina. For her first teaching contract, Cone recalled, "We were paid $60 a month for eight months, and it was paid in South Carolina scrip," following a common Depression–era practice of paying employ-

Senior Class

BONNIE CONE
LODGE, S. C.

*B.S.  Mathematics*

Y. W. C. A., '25-'28; Y. W. A., '25-'28; Y. W. A.
Circle Leader, '28; Y. W. A. Council, '28; Athletic
Association, '25-'28; Junior-Freshman Field Ball
Team, '25; Class Hockey Team, '26-'28; Class Bas-
ketball Team, '28; Class Swimming Team '28;
Class Track Team, '28; Class Crew, '26-'28; Math-
ematics Club, '26-'28; Science Club, '26-'28; Secre-
tary-Treasurer Science Club, '27; President Science
Club, '28; Vice-President Mathematics Club, '27;
President Mathematics Club, '28; Dining Room
Proctor-in-Chief, '28; Executive Board, '28; Presi-
dents' Forum, '28.

Bonnie is our good angel, a person of such a many sided personality one never can accurately
say what she is.  A Math shark, a science fiend—but then, is there anything Bonnie can't do?
As president of the Math and Science Clubs she has served quite ably this year.  She is also
a splendid athlete.  Her excellent work as guard on the basketball team and her remarkable
dexterity with the hockey stick are evidences of her prowess in this line.

Bonnie is a person who radiates calmness and peace.  Her dignified and rather retiring man-
ner covers a spirit of fun and friendliness.  In the midst of rushing college life she is a person
who keeps things steady.  One can go to her and unburden one's troubles.  Bonnie gives us calm
and a new faith in ourselves.  Does Bonnie have many friends?  The question shows you
haven't met her.  Keep your ideals, Bonnie, the world needs you and the spirit you have to give.

The Coker College yearbook (*The Milestone 1928*) called Bonnie "a person who
radiates calmness and peace. In the midst of rushing college life she is a person
who keeps things steady. Bonnie gives us calm and a new faith in ourselves." While
urging her to "keep your ideals," *The Milestone* also asked a more profound and
lasting question: "Is there anything Bonnie *can't* do?" (Emphasis added.)

ees in local currency that did not trade at face value. This meant that if you needed to have money on hand —which, as Cone recalled, everyone she knew did—"You had to discount it." In 1933, Cone left Lake View and took another position at McColl High School in Marlboro County. From there, she taught mathematics at Gaffney High School in 1937 while also attending graduate school at Duke University during the summer, culminating in a master's degree in mathematics in 1941.

By 1940, Cone had built such a notable reputation as a math teacher in South Carolina that the principal of Central High School in Charlotte, Elmer H. Garinger, set out to recruit her. "I had a position at Kannapolis for that fall," she noted. "So when I came for an interview with Dr. Garinger, before I came I said I have another offer. He said, 'I can get you out of that.'" She recalled, "I knew that Central High was one of the finest high schools in the state . . . and I knew Dr. Garinger was an outstanding principal."

The ensuing job negotiation was an early test of Cone's skill at persuasion. She enjoyed teaching a range of concepts, so during her interview for the position, she declined Garinger's initial offer to teach only one subject. She told Garinger, "I don't want to teach plane geometry all day long, or college algebra. I'd like five different preparations." He responded that he would accommodate this request if she taught a course in business math, to which she agreed. "Dr. Garinger answered all my questions and met all my needs," so she joined the faculty of Central High, hired by Garinger on her terms.

## World War II

But labor shortages in 1943 offered a new opportunity. The nation had entered World War II, and with many male teachers serving in the armed forces and deployed overseas, there was a shortage of faculty for Duke University's military training program. In 1942, the American Council on Education had issued a report on how to best use colleges and universities in the war effort, as many of them were already facing precipitous drops in enrollment due to many college-age men having joined the military.

Out of this report was born the Navy's V-12 College Training Program, which was designed to supplement the number of commissioned naval officers during the war. Those eligible included enlisted personnel recommended by their commanding officer, Navy and Marine ROTC members, and eventually high school applicants who could pass a qualifying exam. The program also paid tuition to participating colleges and universities for college courses taught to qualified candidates. The V-12 program began operation on July 1, 1943, at 131 colleges and universities. In North Carolina, the program was hosted at the University of North Carolina at Chapel Hill, Wake Forest College (now University) in Winston-Salem, and Duke University in Durham.

The Navy soon discovered that, across the board, the trainees' skills in areas like math and science were lacking—so much so that they were not making passing grades. In his study of the history of the V-12 program, Henry C. Herge notes that "this problem was solved by dedicated faculty members who were imbued with a strong patriotism" and a personal desire to contribute to the war effort. They gave freely of their time, tutoring trainees individually or in groups. "This kind of dedication," Herge argues, "salvaged many who continued in good standing in the program once over the hurdle."

In this way Cone contributed to the war effort and became the only woman to teach in Duke's V-12 program. Positions typically held by men were filled by women during the war, and the V-12 program was no exception. Seeking teachers with the required skills and dedication, the chairman of the mathematics department at Duke, John Gergen, contacted Cone for help. Cone accepted the position with the understanding that she could return to Central High later. Yet once there, Cone's skill at teaching math continued to attract attention, propelling her further from a typical path for a female schoolteacher during this time. In the spring of 1945, Cone was even called on to work in Washington, DC, with the Statistical Division of the Naval Ordnance Laboratory. Recalling this move, she said, "Well, it was war too and you had to have some sense of loyalty to your country. If there's something there that you should be doing, you'd better get there and do it, . . . I did what I could do." She stayed in that position until August 1946, working with data used in the detection and laying of mines.

After her service to the nation, Cone was ready to return to her students at Central High. "I had promised Dr. Garinger, when I left in the summer of 1943, that I would return to my high school teaching," she recalled. She did return, but as fate would have it, she was not quite finished with her work educating servicemen.

## Charlotte Center

After the war, the profound effects on American society brought changes to Central High. The Servicemen's Readjustment Act of 1944—known as the GI Bill—provided many benefits for returning veterans, including funds to attend college. In 1946, North Carolina faced a dilemma resulting from the large numbers of returning veterans who wished to take advantage of these benefits. State leaders realized that, if early indications were accurate, enrollment demand would soon outstrip supply, and many of the applicants would be denied admittance to college. Under the direction of Governor R. Gregg Cherry, a steering committee comprising many of the state's leading educators was formed to develop a plan to provide educational access for all qualified applicants.

The committee arrived at the idea that the best way to meet the surge in demand was through the development of a system of off-campus university extension centers offering the equivalent of the freshman year. At the minimum, this plan bought the Consolidated University (consisting of the three campuses that existed at that time: UNC Chapel Hill, North Carolina State University, and Woman's College of the University of North Carolina, later renamed University of North Carolina at Greensboro) time to prepare additional options, especially if the extent of the predicted surge in enrollment turned out to be accurate. The Extension Division of the University of North Carolina was given the initial administrative responsibility for the centers, with the North Carolina College Conference lending support and sponsorship to the program shortly after it began in November 1946. The original twelve centers were located in Albemarle, Burlington, Burnsville, Charlotte, Fayetteville, Gastonia, Goldsboro, Greensboro, Hendersonville, Murphy, Rocky Mount, and Wilmington. In 1947, the North Carolina College Conference also approved the addition of sophomore-year courses at the centers where this was necessitated by demand. The Charlotte Center opened in Central High School on September 23, 1946, and offered evening classes primarily to servicemen returning from the war.

As associate superintendent of the Charlotte school system as well as principal of Central High, Garinger was responsible for securing a director for the center. He had two in mind for the position: Charles Bernard, a doctoral student from Chapel Hill, and math instructor Bonnie Cone. Reasoning that Bernard's gender would foster a quick rapport among a student body com-

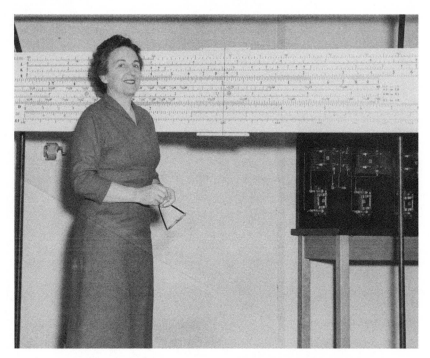

The Mathematician: Cone standing beside her slide rule.

posed predominantly of men, Garinger chose Bernard to head up the center for the first year. Cone, nevertheless, was plenty busy during 1946 and 1947, teaching her full high school workload during the day, then teaching part time and assisting Bernard at Charlotte Center in the evening.

It was here that Cone began a longstanding practice of putting in eighteen-hour workdays, according to many who knew her at the time. She recalled, "In addition to a full load of teaching at the high school with mathematics in the tenth, eleventh, and twelfth grades, I was asked to do all of the testing for the center, and I taught seven hours a week, which was considerable." She admitted, "I don't know how many hours" she worked, "but I know there weren't any left for anything except high school [and] college work."

## CHAPTER 2

# A Dream Takes Root

"It seemed to me it was constant, quarter after quarter. You just wondered, will it continue the next quarter? Chapel Hill could pull the plug and say 'no, don't continue.' We knew that." —Bonnie Cone

WHEN CONE RETURNED TO Central High in August 1947, she received three pieces of unexpected news from Garinger. The first concerned Charles Bernard's abrupt resignation as the director of Charlotte Center to return to Chapel Hill to finish his doctorate. "I had no warning at all really," she recalled. "Charlie gave us none. . . . School was supposed to start in about a month, and we were adding the sophomore year." However, before she could process this news, Garinger delivered the second like a full broadside: She was taking over as director.

This shocked Cone—she was a math teacher, not an administrator. She had never taken on those types of responsibilities. "I protested," Cone remembered of the conversation, "but he said it wouldn't do any good. . . . You have to do this." In an attempt to lessen the blow, Garinger promised her that the assignment was only temporary. Resigned to her fate, Cone accepted the position because, as she explained later in a speech, "When the chief tells you this, the man who brought you to this community, who had the confidence and trust in you, you have to. You can't do otherwise." She found the director's "office": a small room, with "Lost and Found" inscribed on the door. By her description, the office included "one homemade desk—probably no more than twenty-four by thirty-six inches—that had no drawers [and] just one shelf. I had a beautiful two-drawer file which had been bought the year before, so it was nearly new, and one discarded Royal typewriter."

Administrator: Cone at her desk as the director of Charlotte College.

Then the third piece of unexpected news arrived: Nothing was ready for the upcoming year. Cone speculated that the reason for this stemmed from Bernard thinking that the center would not open in the fall, thus his resignation and return to Chapel Hill. "We had really no teachers recruited—this was a month before school opened—and less than forty students [signed up for the fall quarter]." It was here that one might have caught the first glimpse of Cone's potential as an administrator, because in less than a month she was able to recruit more than 250 additional students, plus the faculty required to instruct them.

As director, Cone persistently pushed for things she thought the center needed, such as smaller classes, summer school, and increased pay for instructors. She even successfully advocated for a raise in her own salary, pointing out that she made less than a high school teacher who only taught one class at the center. "I had to give up my high school teaching," she explained, "but my day started at exactly the same time. I was there from the time the building opened at eight o'clock or eight-thirty in the morning, and my day just continued right on up until ten o'clock. I was there every night until . . . usually ten-thirty or eleven, and at registration time it might be two or three in the morning. They were long, hard days, but you had the feeling that you were doing something that really was important."

She also put together an advisory committee to provide guidance for the center. "I knew we had the local school board," said Cone, "but I knew they had too many other things to do, and I believe we needed somebody who was interested particularly in us." To lead the group, she reached out to J. Murrey Atkins, chair of the Charlotte School Board, who agreed to chair it. "I'm a little surprised that I was able to move that fast, but certainly I felt the need to be able to move and try to put together a group of that sort. I'm glad we did it."

From the outset, Charlotte was the largest of the extension centers. The number of students served at the Charlotte Center consistently outpaced that of the others, and the perception that there was a need for publicly supported higher education in the city rose with each record-breaking enrollment. However, the extension centers were designed to be temporary. C. E. McIntosh, assistant director of the college centers for the Extension Division of the University of North Carolina, further underscored this seeming inevitability when he assured the 1947 North Carolina College Conference that, regardless of the addition of the sophomore year, when student applications returned to a level that the three universities could manage without the extension centers, the centers would have served their purpose and would be discontinued.

This troubled Cone, because "she saw what college meant to these students who usually had to work a full day before coming to school and they were in danger of losing their gateway to a better life," writes Mary Snead Boger in *Charlotte 23*. By the end of 1948, the possibility of that reality seemed inevitable when the Extension Division announced that the existing colleges could handle the overflow, the emergency was over, and the remaining centers—including Charlotte—would close permanently on July 1, 1949.

## Charlotte College

Cone described 1949 as "a year of crisis, a year of decision." As it had consistently been the largest extension center in terms of enrollment since its

Central High School, the first location of Charlotte College.

inception, it did not seem—from many Charlotteans' point of view—that the need for access to publicly supported higher education had waned to the point where closing was warranted. Talk began of creating a two-year junior college out of the center because, as Cone had told the *Charlotte Observer* in 1948, "something definite should be done to establish the institution as a permanent thing." Consulting with her advisory board, they were in agreement that the need in Charlotte for access to higher education was real and in danger of slipping away if the center closed. In response, Atkins, in consultation with legal counsel from the city and the local school board, drafted a bill allowing the Charlotte school system to take over and operate the center.

The General Assembly gave its approval on April 4, 1949, creating the Charlotte Community College System, with the newly named Charlotte College as its centerpiece. As this was still the era of Jim Crow segregation, a separate institution, Carver College, was established to serve Black students at Second Ward High School. The recently passed legislation provided initial funding for the schools and provided a mechanism by which to secure more when needed. "We got $10,000 for non-tax money for each institution, and that was to supplement tuition and fees," recalled Cone. "And when that proved inadequate, that we could then ask that we be permitted to go to the voters to vote up to . . . five cents on the $100 property evaluation." Cone was forever grateful that the crisis occurred in 1949, an odd-numbered year, because the legislature was in session. "If it had been an even-numbered year, we would have just died. . . . There would have been no way out."

After submitting proof that Charlotte College aligned with junior college principles, among other tasks, Cone was rewarded in May 1950, when the college was notified by state authorities that Charlotte College "may now be recognized as a standard junior college as of the academic year 1949–50." This designation allowed students to transfer their credits to other senior-level institutions. Cone personally recruited students for the college whenever opportunity arose. "I tried to visit every school in the cities and counties— Mecklenburg County schools and Charlotte City schools," adding that she "wanted to talk to the folks that were not planning to go to college; those who had not chosen. I didn't want to talk to the people who knew they were going to Chapel Hill, Duke, Davidson, or whatever. I wanted to tell those students who could not make plans to go to college that we would be here," because "what we were after was not to let a student who had ability to go to school be denied that opportunity just because of lack of money. . . . We had an institution available to them."

While the Board of School Commissioners was granted permission in 1951 to recognize the college as a four-year institution, the board decided against it, choosing to stay a two-year junior college for the foreseeable future due to concerns over financial sustainability: The $10,000 received in 1949 was a one-time disbursement, not a recurring funding source. Cone managed the school well enough on that and monies collected from student tuition and fees, but by 1954 it was becoming a losing battle. Cone "knew we were getting in the red." The initial disbursement spent, and with tuition and fees not covering the widening shortfall, "I don't know how we stayed alive," she recalled, and "I don't see how we could have gone on" following the same trend.

The school system was also in the middle of a postwar building program as it raced to meet Charlotte's booming school-age population—it had no extra income to give, so asking for more money for the college through an increase in property taxes was initially off the table. However, by March 1954, that view had changed. School Board Commissioner Ben S. Horack was quoted in the *Charlotte Observer* stating that a tax levy "was a matter of compelling necessity if the colleges (Charlotte and Carver) are to survive." The election

Cone, working with her secretaries at Charlotte College, circa 1955.

was held May 18. Ironically, a campaign event that day brought Dwight D. Eisenhower to Freedom Park, causing less than three thousand voters to head to the polls: a mere 4.3 percent voter turnout. Still, the levy passed by more than six hundred votes.

Members of the advisory board, in particular local businessman and engineer Woodford A. "Woody" Kennedy, saw an opportunity emerging: the chance to turn Charlotte College into a full-fledged, and state-supported, university. With the aim of garnering wide backing for this endeavor, Cone continued to build strong relationships throughout the community, advocating for the importance of publicly supported higher education and touting the potential economic impact of a four-year public institution in Charlotte. Jack Claiborne, journalist and former associate vice chancellor of public relations for the university, recalled that she was very good at getting through to people: "I've heard businessmen say Bonnie would come in and they would steel themselves, ready to say no. Then they'd sit down . . . she'd start talking . . . and then they'd wind up saying yes."

By 1956, momentum began to reach a critical mass when the Chamber of Commerce endorsed moving Charlotte College out of Central High School to its own location, which had yet to be determined. A year later, the Community College Act allowed the college to begin offering day classes, and

W.A. Kennedy, considered the spiritual father of Charlotte College and an unflagging advocate for state support. Kennedy was one of the first to see the need for publicly supported higher education in Charlotte and found an ally in Cone. He died on May 11, 1958, on the eve of what would have been his installation as a trustee of Charlotte Community College System.

its enrollment of 492 students surpassed two of North Carolina's four-year colleges! Nineteen fifty-seven was indeed, as Cone noted later, "a year when tremendous activity was taking place."

The passage of the 1957 act set the stage for two years of raising capital improvement funds through bond referendums. The first, occurring in April 1958, extended the two-cent city tax that funded the college, levying it on the whole of Mecklenburg County. A second referendum in November saw Charlotte voters approve a statewide bond by a three-to-one margin, providing $975,000 in state matching funds beginning in 1959. One year later,

Charlotte College and Carver College Board of Trustees, June 1963:
Tom Belk, James Alexander, Addison Reese, Jack Delaney, Paul Lucas,
Bonnie Cone, J. Murrey Atkins, Sheldon Smith, Oliver Rowe, Linn Garibaldi,
S.J. McCoy, Thomas Watkins. Partially obscured: Ernest A. Beaty

county voters also approved a second bond referendum of $975,000 for the
second phase of the campus-building program.

Through each campaign, Cone was writing letters, making phone calls,
and giving speeches in support of the bonds to a large swath of the county's
civic organizations and electorate, never ceasing to push her vision of what
Charlotte College could be. Said Cone: "As we worked to get the local tax
support and bond support, we could actually see the increase in the voters'
approvals."

On February 2, 1959, Charlotte College literally gained immense ground
when the Board of Trustees purchased 274 acres of land on Highway 49.
The selection of this site, a move heavily influenced by Kennedy, was widely
viewed as strategic, particularly since it would attract commuter students
from many surrounding cities. "We could never have put together that big

parcel of land if we hadn't had a man with Woody Kennedy's vision," recalled Cone. Ever a forward thinker, Kennedy was especially prescient in this regard, as he began buying options on parcels as early as 1951, cobbling together 274 acres in the Mallard Creek area of Mecklenburg County. "If the site is chosen for the campus," he told Cone, "the Trustees can have it for what I paid for it." Conversely, if another site was chosen, Kennedy instructed Cone that the acreage was "to be sold for the maximum and the profits put into the Scholarship Fund."

Cone saw Charlotte College's achievement in securing the land as just the next step toward the goal of achieving university status. She admitted that she was not sanguine with the 1957 Community College Act initially due to the fact "it was only for programs which transferred to senior colleges." So while it was state funding, it was not funding for a four-year institution. But the legislation called for the existing junior colleges of the state to "relinquish their bonds with the local school boards and to come under the jurisdiction of the State Board of Higher Education," which offered some advantages in terms of a funding source. Cone understood the local school system was straining to meet demand and that not having to fund a junior college would go a long way toward accomplishing their goals. "They had lots of responsibility with those 'war babies.' They needed to be building more public school buildings," and "we needed to get on our own."

But the experiences working under state control during the Charlotte Center era made Cone reticent. And she was not alone in her reservations, as leaders of the state's other junior colleges joined her in voicing their concern. However, as she would relate years later, securing state support ultimately outweighed these considerations. "I knew we were taking one half a loaf but," acknowledging that some state support was better than none at all, "we decided to take it."

While Cone was working to drum up support for the college, she was gaining recognition in her profession as well. In 1959, noting that she was "one of the few women administrative heads of coeducational colleges, private or community," the Southern Association of Junior Colleges elected her president of their organization—the first woman to ever hold that title. In 1961 she received two honorary degrees on the same day: a doctor of literature degree from her alma mater, Coker College, and an honorary doctorate from Davidson College, another first for a woman. Later that summer the Charlotte Community College Board also conferred upon Cone the title of

The groundbreaking ceremony for the new campus in northeast Mecklenburg County, November 21, 1960. Pictured are Cone; Addison Reese, chair of the Charlotte College site committee; L.P. McLendon, North Carolina Board of Higher Education chair and principal speaker at the ceremony; and J. Murrey Atkins Sr., chairman of the Charlotte College Board of Trustees.

Two Visionaries: Cone standing with Elmer H. Garinger (center right) and others who participated in the groundbreaking ceremony, November 21, 1960.

Cone looks on as the J. Murrey Atkins Library building is constructed, circa 1960–61.

Bonnie Cone and Oliver Rowe at the Charlotte Civitan Club where she won its
Distinguished Citizenship Award in 1965. A Charlotte native and industrialist,
Rowe had a vision for Charlotte College that matched Cone's. He was instrumental
in securing the first major donation for Charlotte College from the Celanese
Corporation and served as a member of both the Charlotte College and University
of North Carolina at Charlotte Board of Trustees.

"president" of Charlotte College, rewarding her hard work and dedication
with an official title. As she began her first year as the official president of the
college, events transpiring in Raleigh would soon prove the final catalyst to
realizing her vision.

## University Status

The following decade brought changes to how North Carolina operated its
colleges and universities that affected Charlotte College's trajectory. Elected
governor in 1960 under a platform promising quality education for North
Carolina, Terry Sanford was very aware of the fact that the 1957 Community

Bonnie Cone with the hand carved "Original 49er," given to her as a gift, 1966.

Cone speaking at the inaugural University Forum, March 2, 1966.
The brainchild of Professor of Political Science Edyth Winningham, the
University Forum was designed to bring distinguished speakers to the university
to hear about the pertinent issues of the day. Entitled "The University and
the Development of the Modern City," this first forum helped
establish the university's urban-oriented focus.

College Act had brought forth a range of important policy questions about
how community colleges would be created and operated moving forward.
In order to come up with a plan, he appointed a twenty-five-member commission, which included Cone and was chaired by attorney Irving Carlyle, a
former state senator from Winston-Salem. "The Carlyle Commission," as it
came to be known, made sixty-one specific recommendations on how to im-
prove higher education in the state when presenting its findings in December
1962. One of those included converting Charlotte College into a four-year
senior institution by adding the junior and senior years in 1963 and 1964,
respectively. That recommendation, adopted by the General Assembly in
May 1963, finally gave Charlotte—and Bonnie Cone—the four-year state-
supported institution that the region needed.

However, another recommendation proved even more fortuitous for the
school, as it authorized the Consolidated Board of Trustees to establish ad-

October 30, 1961: Students launch a campaign to support the November 7, 1961 bond election in front of the Science and Education (Kennedy) Building at Charlotte College. While the referendum was defeated statewide, Mecklenburg County voted overwhelmingly in support of its community college. Out of this defeat came the Carlyle Commission, which helped move the needle forward on Charlotte College's push to become a university.

ditional campuses of the university under conditions prescribed by the board and requiring new campuses to be established "only where there is a clear need for the types of programs that only a university should offer." To that end, the board authorized education scholar Arnold K. King to undertake a study on the expansion of the university with an eye toward Charlotte College as a possible candidate. Completed in October 1964, King's study recommended that "the Board of Trustees of the university, subject to the provisions of General Statute 116-2.1, take appropriate action to make Charlotte College the fourth campus of the University of North Carolina." The report's conclusions helped swiftly secure approval from the Consolidated University Board of Trustees and the State Board of Higher Education, and by January 1965, the final approval was in the hands of the General Assembly.

Pierre Macy, professor of French and chair of the foreign languages
department, leads the way as President Bonnie Cone and the only graduating
class of four-year Charlotte College heads to commencement in 1965.

Back at Charlotte College, Cone was working with her colleagues to build
up the faculty as it transitioned into a four-year institution. With the youth of
the school and its lack of facilities serving as roadblocks to successfully recruit
distinguished faculty, Cone constantly related to them a vision of "the college
as it would be rather than as it was—a handful of buildings alongside a barn
and silo in a former cow pasture." Her approach was successful; one example
is Sherman Burson. Recruited to develop the chemistry program by Cone,
he initially turned down the job offer citing lack of facilities on campus. But
Cone was determined to change his mind, persisting until he finally accepted,
Burson told *UNC Charlotte* magazine in 2003: "It was a hard sell, but clothed
in such a disarming and friendly approach, it didn't seem that way at all." That
initially hesitant chemistry professor ultimately spent his entire career at the
school, retiring in 1985 as the dean of the College of Arts and Sciences.

Other distinguished early faculty recruited by this method included Robert Wallace (English), James Wahab (mathematics), Howard Harlan (sociology), Dan Morrill (history), and Loy Witherspoon (religious studies). In every instance, it was Cone's vision for the college that won them over. None of the faculty recruited by Cone were surprised when Charlotte College developed into the University of North Carolina at Charlotte. As Ken Sanford, the university's first director of public information, writes, "all had seen the picture of the future as painted by Bonnie Cone in 1963–64."

In February 1965, the legislation to make Charlotte College the fourth campus of the University of North Carolina was introduced in the General Assembly. Everything was going well; the legislation passed the Senate without issue, but, according to Ken Sanford, "on the eve of the key vote in the House, the effort somehow hit a snag." Cone, who was in Raleigh to support the bill, was approached by a representative of Governor Dan K. Moore who told her that Moore wanted the legislation withdrawn because he had been informed there were not enough votes to pass it. As he had just assumed office in January, he was not keen to lose his first legislative battle in such a short time. "This was pretty much a shock to me," said Cone. "Representative Jim Vogler was sure and the other legislators from our delegation were sure they had the support needed to pass it in the House."

Vogler, who introduced the bill as head of the Mecklenburg County delegation to the General Assembly, was able to convince Moore to postpone the vote until the following Tuesday so he could check his vote count. This precipitated a flurry of weekend telephone calls from Cone to everyone she knew with legislative connections because "after it was determined that we did have the votes to pass it in the House, we had to be sure that the governor was persuaded to let the bill be taken to the House." The problem, she quipped, was that "every single soul seemed to be in Florida fishing." Not giving up, she kept dialing until she reached banking executive George Broadrick, who agreed to speak with Governor Moore and then meet Cone in Raleigh the next day. After meeting with the governor, Broadrick met Cone at the Sir Walter Raleigh Hotel where he told her that Moore was with them and the legislation would be voted on the following day.

The vote was crucial; Cone described Tuesday, March 2, 1965, as "the longest day I ever lived." As the culmination of an almost nineteen-year mission, every second leading up to the final vote count must have stretched to forever

Editorial cartoon drawn by Eugene Payne, published in the *Charlotte Observer* on
July 1, 1965, celebrating Bonnie Cone's success in getting Charlotte College elevated
to university status. Courtesy of the *Charlotte Observer*.

and back again in her mind. But any worry she had was quashed when the bill
finally passed on its third reading. As the old bell rang on the Charlotte College campus to celebrate the news, Cone and her staff began the trek back to
Charlotte. As they approached the campus, they noticed it darker than usual,
and drove onto campus to investigate. As Ken Sanford recounts, "suddenly
lights came on everywhere and a shout went up. A student stepped forward

Cone, holding back tears, is surprised by an impromptu celebration
in her name after returning from Raleigh on March 2, 1965.

and placed a bouquet of red roses in Cone's arms. Her eyes glistened with
tears. Then she was instructed to follow the crowd to the student center,
where music was playing and students were dancing, and a gala impromptu
celebration ensued."

## The Selection of a Chancellor

On July 1, 1965, Charlotte College became the University of North Carolina
at Charlotte, with Cone named as acting chancellor until a permanent one
was selected. That same month, Cone was featured in a *Time* magazine profile entitled "The School Miss Bonnie Built." In that article, the magazine
asked: "With its future growth seemingly assured, the big question for the
campus now is: Will Miss Bonnie, who is acting Chancellor, be appointed
permanently?" The article also wondered whether "her sex and her lack of

an earned doctorate might be considered handicaps" for her chances. Cone appeared to brush those questions aside as the fall approached, focusing on the school's first semester as a university.

Since Cone had been director and president of Charlotte College, and was already considered the founder of the university, many expected she should naturally be named chancellor. However, Dean W. Colvard—the president of Mississippi State University and a North Carolina native who had a deep history with NC State—was the final choice for the first official chancellor. This decision sparked a public controversy.

While it is true that Cone never obtained an earned doctorate as Colvard had, by 1965 she had already received the first three of ten honorary doctorates awarded her during her lifetime for her outstanding achievements. It is also worth noting that at this time other chancellors lacking earned doctorates led universities in the North Carolina system, but these were men—there had never been a female chancellor. Controversies rarely have straightforward explanations, which is illustrated by the thoughts of people who knew Cone.

Cone's close friend, Loy Witherspoon, was among those who believed her gender worked against her becoming chancellor. "I think she began to sense that she was not going to be made the chancellor," he recalled. "In fact Mr. (Ross) Puette told me that she'll never be made chancellor." When he pressed Puette, an early benefactor of Charlotte Center and Charlotte College, the latter said Cone's gender was the primary factor. Witherspoon, pointing out that was illegal, was rebuffed when Puette told him point blank: "They don't know that around here." Witherspoon believed she had the backing of her students and the greater Charlotte community to get the job, but they were not the ones driving that decision. "The sad thing is," he said, ". . . the people from the faculty [who] were appointed to go meet with a subcommittee to choose the chancellor didn't support her," and "that just broke my heart."

Many who worked closely with Cone considered her hands-on, individualized approach an immense strength in many respects, but a weakness for a university chancellor. Claiborne explained: "A great many people, like John Paul Lucas, Pete McKnight, Addison Reese, etc. thought Bonnie had a 'tea party' kind of style. [She] was the kind of administrator who might go around the edges of the student prom dance and smell the cups to make sure there was no alcohol in them. They thought she had too narrow a perspective on student life. Truth was, Bonnie's perspective on student life was wider than theirs."

Many believed Colvard's experience and credentials were the primary reasons he was chosen for chancellor. Although Claiborne felt Cone's gender was a factor in the decision, he also felt the university would not have had the same ascent without Colvard's expertise. Dan Morrill, retired professor of history, believed Colvard was the safe choice. Leaders were very worried about meeting the standards of the other three chancellors in the university system; they wanted validity and a certain, smooth transition.

William Friday, the president of the University of North Carolina system at the time, said in 2012 that he had been following tradition when appointing a man with a PhD and a tested reputation as a university chancellor, and he believed Colvard handled the job well. But he expressed regret that he had not made Cone chancellor. While he still maintained Cone was not the best qualified, generally speaking, to lead a university, he said she should have been made the first chancellor of UNC Charlotte out of respect and fairness to her: "You've got to acknowledge that when somebody spends their lifetime building something, you ought to do everything you can to be fair about that."

Some of those close to Cone believed she was deeply disappointed in not being chosen for chancellor, but she never revealed it to them. "There was no doubt she was disappointed," recalled Witherspoon, "the lightness-of-heart she always had seemed to go away." Claiborne remembered that Cone disappeared for a while afterward, which was very unusual for her.

Since she was known to redirect any conversation about herself toward the university, we can never know exactly how she felt about the chancellor controversy, but we can consider the few relevant statements she made. When offered the position of vice chancellor by Friday in 1966, she expressed her appreciation but politely declined, explaining, "I sincerely believe it is in the best interest of the institution that our new chancellor have the maximum opportunity to choose the staff who will assist him in the big task which he assumes." When specifically asked about the chancellorship, she replied, "In my heart of hearts, it was not a problem." Cone also explained that she simply did not have the time to work toward a doctorate, a sentiment that was echoed by others including Friday.

One thing is certain: Cone's thoughts were always centered on the uni-

Cone walks with Dean W. Colvard as William Friday, president of the
University of North Carolina System, leads the way during Colvard's installation
as the first chancellor of UNC Charlotte. The event was held on March 3, 1967,
the second anniversary of gaining university status.

versity. "Nobody here is worried about the future, and I least of all," she told
*Time*. "We are not here to elevate ourselves, but the institution." Upon the
appointment of Colvard as chancellor, Cone continued her service to the
university by accepting the position of vice chancellor of student and alumni
affairs, the title of which was changed later to vice chancellor for student
affairs and community relations.

CHAPTER 3

# Legacy

"She is one of the most memorable people whom I have ever known
and the single beyond my own family to whom I owe the most."
—M. S. Mahaley Jr., MD, UNC Charlotte alumnus

I N BUILDING THE UNIVERSITY, the people—especially her students—
were always Cone's first priority. It is evident in her correspondence
throughout her career, and into retirement, that she single-handedly
changed the lives of thousands of people. When those who have met Cone
are asked about her direct influence, they invariably provide a description
similar to that offered by former student Douglas Biddy, who became a member of the university's Board of Trustees in 1973:

> She had the capacity to make each student feel that we were special to
> her and therefore a special person indeed. . . . If I, being but a grain of
> sand in her beach of life, was so affected by her teaching and friendship,
> I can hardly envision the multitude of lives she has touched over the
> years. She had the capacity to bring out the very best in the very least,
> no small task.

Indeed, Cone deeply influenced many students who later held notable careers
in law, medicine, business, journalism, and other fields.

Author William Styron, best known for his novel *Sophie's Choice*, was a
student of Cone's when she taught in Duke University's V-12 program. In
response to seeing Cone's profile in *Time*, Styron wrote to congratulate her in
1965. In the letter, he recalled a day that Cone called him out in class as he was
engrossed in a novel instead of paying attention. Styron wrote, "I said I was
going to be a writer come hell or high water and I remember you said with

41

Cone counsels student, circa 1959.

great good humor that you hoped I would succeed in my ambition, adding that when my first novel came out you hoped I would send you a copy to your home." He enclosed a copy of his first book, *Lie Down in Darkness.*

In 1988 Cone was nominated for the Nancy Susan Reynolds Award, which "recognized the unsung heroes of North Carolina whose vision, determination, resourcefulness and strength of character caused them to make a positive difference in the state." A lengthy nomination booklet demonstrates Cone's immense impact. Several former students wrote enthusiastic nomination letters, which further highlight Cone's almost unbelievable dedication to her students.

Two of the letters are from alumni who went on to careers in medicine. M. S. Mahaley Jr., MD, who attended Charlotte College in 1951 and 1952, and whose parents had not attended college, described Cone's profound impact on the trajectory of his life. "There is no doubt in my mind," he wrote, "that without her encouragement and direction, I would never have even considered it possible to go to college nor would I have approached a college education with the seriousness that I think subsequently permitted me to move forward in my professional career through additional education, medical school, and residency."

Ronald Caldwell, MD, described how, as the great-grandson of a formerly enslaved person, he and his wife benefited immensely from Cone's personal encouragement when he attended UNC Charlotte from 1967 to 1971. He also wrote that she supported Black student activists who demonstrated on campus for civil rights: "Certainly, at that time, swift administrative action to suppress student unrest would have been more popular and had more community support than the role taken by Dr. Cone, who supported a 'less-fortunate group' who chose to challenge the system and make it more responsive to the entire community."

In her letter, entrepreneur Bonnie B. Thyer, who started her own company in the male-dominated field of specialty advertising, described Cone as her mentor and role model: "I felt that if Bonnie E. Cone could operate at the highest levels in her profession, there was no reason why I could not be successful in my chosen field." This sentiment supports what Loy Witherspoon recalled later about her impact on the ambitions of women who knew her: "I think she became an example to other women that you could do it."

CONE HAD AN ENORMOUS impact on colleagues as well as students. In June 1997, on the occasion of her ninetieth birthday, Cone received a plethora of letters and a celebration was held on campus. Many of those she hired or worked with during the early stages of the college's development wrote or gave a speech in her honor. Those colleagues thought back to the early years or commented on her character and ability:

> "Your many friends and admirers are well aware that you have a particular way of bringing people together—both humanly and physically." —Chancellor Emeritus E. K. Fretwell

> "Your mystical ability to see the future and convey that vision to others, including me, was a real gift." —Ken Sanford

> "Your vision and your stark, 'unblinking' courage astounded me then even as they continue to epitomize you today." —Loy Witherspoon

Professor Emeritus of History Edward Perzel recalled, "No one ever said no to Miss Bonnie. It was not because one feared her but because her positive

outlook and energy swept you up and did not let go." Perzel also remembered discussing the history of UNC Charlotte with Cone for the Freshman
Leadership program: "To watch the looks of appreciation and reverence that
appeared on the faces of the freshman leaders, as they grasped the enormity of
this lady's presence, is a treasured memory. They understood that few people,
in a lifetime, could walk out their front door, look around, and realize what
they surveyed was all there because of their leadership. The women in the
class beamed with the recognition of what Bonnie accomplished in a 'man's
world' where then most women feared to tread."

The same inspiring and persuasive nature that allowed Cone to gain allies
in building UNC Charlotte also motivated students, both men and women,
to enroll in college, finish their degrees, and strive to be their absolute best in
their chosen careers.

"Bonnie Cone really was a very remarkable human being."
—William Friday

CONE OFFICIALLY RETIRED FROM UNC Charlotte on June 30, 1973, but that does not mean she began to slow down. Upon her retirement, the university bestowed on Cone the title of vice chancellor emeritus to recognize her distinguished career. While she no longer put in eighteen-hour days, she continued to be very involved in the community and on campus, working part-time for the Office of Development and the Foundation of UNC Charlotte from 1973 to 1977. At the age of eighty-two, her ambition remained strong as she ran for a seat on the Board of Governors. Although she was not elected to that seat, she continued to remain active on campus until she was physically unable, often attending campus events—such as basketball games and alumni events—and doing anything she could to support the university.

In a 1987 letter, C. D. Spangler Jr. let her know that her influence indirectly continued to support the college: "Even now we learn that Nordica Adelaide Jamieson has left her estate to the University. She did so specifically because she admired you and what you were doing. I suspect, while you never knew her, she probably knew you quite well." A 1982 article from the *Charlotte Weekly South* considers the fact that Cone never married. Cone is quoted as saying, "My mother said I never had time for it. Perhaps I didn't, but I guess you can make time for anything." And children? Through her eyes, Cone had thousands of children, and they were the students and alumni of the University of North Carolina at Charlotte.

Cone, between Charlotte businessman and second president
of the University of North Carolina System, C.D. Spangler (left), and
Professor of Philosophy and Religious Studies Loy Witherspoon (right),
one of her closest friends and confidants.

It was through that lens that Chancellor James H. Woodward conceived of a unique way to both honor Cone while also leaving no doubt as to her importance to the university. He proposed to the Board of Trustees to have her interred on the campus so she could "oversee her institution in perpetuity." The concept itself was not new, examples of such honors already existed at Duke University and Winthrop University in South Carolina. Woodward acknowledged this but noted, "I do think Bonnie's situation is unique because so few presidents and chancellors devote a professional and personal lifetime to a single institution." Where most presidents and chancellors had families of their own, "UNC Charlotte was Bonnie's family."

The Board of Trustees, being of the same opinion, unanimously endorsed the idea at its December 1996 meeting, and the Board of Governors fol-

Fifty Years of Leadership: Cone with Chancellor Emeritus E.K. Fretwell (sitting), Chancellor Emeritus D.W. Colvard, and Chancellor James H. Woodward in 1994.

lowed. There remained only two issues. The first was regulatory and dealt with the burial of persons on state property. Once determined no exception was needed, Woodward addressed the last issue directly: Cone's permission. With Loy Witherspoon, Woodward visited Cone at her home on the afternoon of March 24, 1997, and presented the idea to her. Bonnie Sawyer, Cone's niece and namesake, informed Woodward the following week her aunt was overwhelmed by the proposal, but also very pleased, and has "accepted your gracious offer."

Bonnie Cone died at the age of ninety-five on March 8, 2003. She is the only person the university has interred on the UNC Charlotte campus. Her stone memorial is in the Van Landingham Glen and reads "Founder The

University of North Carolina at Charlotte." It is inscribed with a quote by American author Edward Everett Hale, the same one on a ceramic tile that Cone kept on her desk:

> I am only one
> But I am one
> I cannot do everything
> But I can do something
> What I can do
> I ought to do
> And what I ought to do
> By the grace of God, I will do

# SOURCES

## Introduction

### Oral History Interviews

Claiborne, Jack. Interviewed by Christina Wright, March 28, 2012. Oral History Collections, J. Murrey Atkins Library, University of North Carolina at Charlotte. https://goldmine.uncc.edu/index/render/object/pid/uncc:2557/parentPID /uncc:bc (accessed June 26, 2020).

Friday, William C. Interviewed by Christina Wright, May 1, 2012. Oral History Collections, J. Murrey Atkins Library, University of North Carolina at Charlotte. https://goldmine.uncc.edu/index/render/object/pid/uncc:2572/parentPID /uncc:bc (accessed June 26, 2020).

Murphy, Harvey. Interviewed by Christina Wright, August 15, 2012. Oral History Collections, J. Murrey Atkins Library, University of North Carolina at Charlotte. https://goldmine.uncc.edu/index/render/object/pid/uncc:2565/parentPID /uncc:bc (accessed June 26, 2020).

Witherspoon, Loy. Interviewed by Christina Wright, June 3, 2010, interview 7. Oral History Collections, J. Murrey Atkins Library, University of North Carolina at Charlotte. https://goldmine.uncc.edu/index/render/object/pid/uncc:1378 /parentPID/uncc:lw (accessed June 26, 2020).

Witherspoon, Loy. Interviewed by Christina Wright, June 8, 2010, interview 8. Oral History Collections, J. Murrey Atkins Library, University of North Carolina at Charlotte. https://goldmine.uncc.edu/index/render/object/pid uncc:1381/parentPID/uncc:lw (accessed June 26, 2020).

## Chapter 1

### Oral History Interviews

Cone, Bonnie E. Interviewed by Edward S. Perzel, December 8, 1987, interview 7. Oral History Collections, J. Murrey Atkins Library, University of North Carolina at Charlotte. https://goldmine.uncc.edu/index/render/object/pid /uncc:2892/parentPID/uncc:cb

Cone, Bonnie E. Interviewed by Ken Sanford, undated (circa 1972), transcript. Bonnie Ethel Cone Papers, MS0112. J. Murrey Atkins Library, University of North Carolina at Charlotte.

Cone, Bonnie E. Interviewed by Ken Sanford, June 13, 1973, interview III, part 2, transcript. Bonnie Ethel Cone Papers, MS0112. J. Murrey Atkins Library, University of North Carolina at Charlotte.

### Archives and Manuscripts

Charlotte College Records, UA0034. J. Murrey Atkins Library, University of North Carolina at Charlotte.

Cone, Bonnie. "Dreams Do Come True" speech, September 13, 1983. Audio-video materials, 1960-2004, UA0077. J. Murrey Atkins Library, University of North Carolina at Charlotte.

Cone (Bonnie Ethel) Papers MS0112. J. Murrey Atkins Library, University of North Carolina at Charlotte.

### Publications

Boger, Mary Snead. "Bonnie Ethel Cone." In *Charlotte 23*, 53–67. Bassett, VA: Bassett Printing Corporation, 1972.

Herge, Henry C. *Navy V-12*. Paducah, KY: Turner Publishing Company, 1996.

Sanford, J. Kenneth. *Charlotte and UNC Charlotte: Growing Up Together*. Charlotte: University of North Carolina at Charlotte, 1996.

Segner III, Kenyon Bertel. *A History of the Community College Movement in North Carolina: 1927–1963*. Kenansville, NC: James Sprunt Press, 1974.

## Chapter 2

### Interviews

Claiborne, Jack. Interviewed by Christina Wright, March 28, 2012. Oral History Collections, J. Murrey Atkins Library, University of North Carolina at Charlotte. https://goldmine.uncc.edu/index/render/object/pid/uncc:2557/parentPID /uncc:bc (accessed June 26, 2020).

Cone, Bonnie E. Interviewed by Ken Sanford, undated (circa 1972), transcript. Bonnie Ethel Cone Papers, MS0112. J. Murrey Atkins Library, University of North Carolina at Charlotte.

Cone, Bonnie E. Interviewed by Ken Sanford, March 7, 1973, transcript, Box 1, Folder 14. Bonnie Ethel Cone Papers, MS0112. J. Murrey Atkins Library, University of North Carolina at Charlotte.

Cone, Bonnie E. Interviewed by Edward S. Perzel, December 17, 1987, interview 8.

Oral History Collections, J. Murrey Atkins Library, University of North Carolina at Charlotte. https://goldmine.uncc.edu/index/render/object/pid /uncc:2903/parentPID/uncc:cb (accessed June 26, 2020).

Cone, Bonnie E. Interviewed by Edward S. Perzel, February 4, 1988, interview 10. Oral History Collections, J. Murrey Atkins Library, University of North Carolina at Charlotte. https://goldmine.uncc.edu/index/render/object/pid /uncc:2905/parentPID/uncc:cb (accessed June 26, 2020).

Cone, Bonnie E. Interviewed by Edward S. Perzel, February 9, 1988, interview 11. Oral History Collections, J. Murrey Atkins Library, University of North Carolina at Charlotte. https://goldmine.uncc.edu/index/render/object/pid /uncc:2896/parentPID/uncc:cb (accessed June 26, 2020).

Cone, Bonnie E. Interviewed by Edward S. Perzel, February 11, 1988, interview 12. Oral History Collections, J. Murrey Atkins Library, University of North Carolina at Charlotte. https://goldmine.uncc.edu/index/render/object/pid /uncc:2898/parentPID/uncc:cb (accessed June 26, 2020).

Cone, Bonnie E. Interviewed by Edward S. Perzel, March 1, 1988, interview 13. Oral History Collections, J. Murrey Atkins Library, University of North Carolina at Charlotte. https://goldmine.uncc.edu/index/render/object/pid/uncc:2901 /parentPID/uncc:cb (accessed June 26, 2020).

Friday, William C. Interviewed by Christina Wright, May 1, 2012. Oral History Collections, J. Murrey Atkins Library, University of North Carolina at Charlotte. https://goldmine.uncc.edu/index/render/object/pid/uncc:2572/parentPID /uncc:bc (accessed June 26, 2020).

Morrill, Dan L. Interviewed by Christina Wright, March 6, 2012, interview 5. Oral History Collections, J. Murrey Atkins Library, University of North Carolina at Charlotte. https://goldmine.uncc.edu/index/render/object/pid/uncc:2574 /parentPID/uncc:bc (accessed June 26, 2020).

Witherspoon, Loy. Interviewed by Christina Wright, June 3, 2010, interview 7. Oral History Collections, J. Murrey Atkins Library, University of North Carolina at Charlotte. https://goldmine.uncc.edu/index/render/object/pid/uncc:1378 parentPID/uncc:lw (accessed June 26, 2020).

### Archives and Manuscripts

Cone (Bonnie Ethel) Papers, MS0112. J. Murrey Atkins Library, University of North Carolina at Charlotte.

Cone, Bonnie. "Dreams Do Come True" speech, September 13, 1983. Audio-video materials, 1960–2004, UA0077. J. Murrey Atkins Library, University of North Carolina at Charlotte.

Charlotte College Records, UA0034. J. Murrey Atkins Library, University of North Carolina at Charlotte.

## Publications

Boger, Mary Snead. "Bonnie Ethel Cone." In *Charlotte 23*, 53-67. Bassett, VA: Bassett Printing Corporation, 1972.

*Charlotte Observer*. "City College Tax Approved At The Polls," May 19, 1954.

*Charlotte Observer*. "How Mecklenburg Voted On Bonds," November 5, 1958.

Collins, Chris. "Miss Cone Is Named President." *Charlotte Collegian* 16, no. 1 (September 18, 1961): 1, 3.

Golden, Harry, Jr. "Vote is Called On Supporting City Colleges." *Charlotte Observer*, March 11, 1954: 1B.

Howard, Gina Carroll. "UNC Charlotte: Bonnie Cone's Promise Fulfilled." *UNC Charlotte* 11, no. 1 (Summer 2003): 11–14.

Leonard, Jerry. "Second Phase Bond Issue Approved." *Charlotte Collegian* 13, no. 3 (December 12, 1960): 1.

McCorkle, Joe E. "The Ballad of Bonnie E. Cone." In *The Annual Report, Rogues and Rascals 1973*, 15. Charlotte: University of North Carolina at Charlotte, 1973.

Rieke, Robert. "A Fragrance of Excellence." In *A Retrospective Vision: The University of North Carolina at Charlotte, 1965–1975*, 49–73. Charlotte: Heritage Printers, Inc., 1977.

Sanford, J. Kenneth. *Charlotte and UNC Charlotte: Growing Up Together.* Charlotte: University of North Carolina at Charlotte, 1996.

Segner III, Kenyon Bertel. *A History of the Community College Movement in North Carolina: 1927-1963.* Kenansville, NC: James Sprunt Press, 1974.

Trotter, Hazel. "Favor Permanent College," *Charlotte Observer*, April 6, 1948.

*Time*. "The School Miss Bonnie Built." July 16, 1965.

# Chapter 3

## Interviews

Claiborne, Jack. Interviewed by Christina Wright, March 28, 2012. Oral History Collections, J. Murrey Atkins Library, University of North Carolina at Charlotte. https://goldmine.uncc.edu/index/render/object/pid/uncc:2557/parentPID/uncc:bc (accessed June 26, 2020).

Witherspoon, Loy. Interviewed by Christina Wright, June 3, 2010, interview 7. Oral History Collections, J. Murrey Atkins Library, University of North Carolina at Charlotte. https://goldmine.uncc.edu/index/render/object/pid/uncc:1378/parentPID/uncc:lw (accessed June 26, 2020).

### *Archives and Manuscripts*

Cone (Bonnie Ethel) Papers, MS0112. J. Murrey Atkins Library, University of North Carolina at Charlotte.

Chancellor (James H. Woodward) Records, 1985–2007, UA0174, University Archives, J. Murrey Atkins Library, University of North Carolina at Charlotte.

## Epilogue

### *Interviews*

Friday, William C. Interviewed by Christina Wright, May 1, 2012. Oral History Collections, J. Murrey Atkins Library, University of North Carolina at Charlotte. https://goldmine.uncc.edu/index/render/object/pid/uncc:2572/parentPID /uncc:bc (accessed June 26, 2020).

Woodward, James H. Informal Conversation with William Jeffers, May 20, 2020.

### *Archives and Manuscripts*

Cone (Bonnie Ethel) Papers, MS0112. J. Murrey Atkins Library, University of North Carolina at Charlotte.

Woodward, James H. Letter to Russell Robinson, October 17, 1996, Chancellor Philip Dubois Records, currently held by the Chancellor's Office. To be transferred to the J. Murrey Atkins Library, University of North Carolina at Charlotte, and made publicly available.

Sawyer, Bonnie Cone. Letter to J. H. Woodward, April 1, 1997. Chancellor Philip Dubois Records, currently held by the Chancellor's Office. To be transferred to the J. Murrey Atkins Library, University of North Carolina at Charlotte, and made publicly available.